Rainforests

A TEMPLAR BOOK
First published in the UK in 2008 by Templar Publishing,
An imprint of The Templar Company plc,
The Granary, North Street,
Dorking,
Surrey,
RH4 1DN
www.templarco.co.uk

Conceived and produced by Weldon Owen Pty Ltd
59-61 Victoria Street, McMahons Point
Sydney, NSW 2060, Australia

WELDON OWEN GROUP
Chairman John Owen

WELDON OWEN PTY LTD
Chief Executive Officer Sheena Coupe
Creative Director Sue Burk
Concept Development John Bull, The Book Design Company
Publishing Coordinator Mike Crowton
Senior Vice President, International Sales Stuart Laurence
Vice President, Sales and New Business Development Amy Kaneko
Vice President, Sales: Asia and Latin America Dawn Low
Administrator, International Sales Kristine Ravn

Project Editor Lesley McFadzean
Art Director Colin Wheatland
Designers Simon Bracken, John Bull/The Book Design Company
Art Manager Trucie Henderson
Illustrators Peter Bull Art Studio, Christer Eriksson, Yvan Meunier/Contact Jupiter

ISBN: 978-1-84011-742-4

Colour reproduction by Chroma Graphics (Overseas) Pte Ltd
Printed by SNP Leefung Printers Ltd
Manufactured in China 5 4 3 2 1

A WELDON OWEN PRODUCTION

▶in*siders*

Rainforests

Richard C. Vogt

templar publishing

Contents

introducing

From Top to Bottom

Plants of the Rainforest

in *focus*

introducing

Rainforest Layers

Tropical rainforests are found in a band across the world between the Tropic of Cancer, north of the Equator, and the Tropic of Capricorn, south of the Equator. Each rainforest itself is divided into vertical bands, or layers. The tallest trees, or emergents, stand above the canopy, and both of these layers are exposed to full sunlight, rain and wind. Beneath the canopy, in the understorey, sunlight is limited, or dappled. There is no wind, but some of the rain falls down from above. The floor, or ground level, of the rainforest is always dark and damp because there is no sunlight and no heat from the sun to dry out the moisture. The plants in each of these layers have adapted in different ways to cope with the very different conditions they face.

Kapok leaves *Growing to a height of 46 metres (150 ft), the kapok tree has compound palmlike leaves of 5–9 leaflets.*

Vines *A tangle of vines, both thick and thin, hang from the branches of canopy and emergent trees.*

Emergent

Canopy

Understorey

Large leaves *Banana leaves in the understorey are very large, to catch what little sunlight there is.*

Floor

Fungi *On the rainforest floor, fungi feed on live or dead plants and dead animals.*

River

Tallest
of the Tall

The tallest trees in the rainforest rise more than 40 metres (130 ft) above the ground. These tall trees appear, or emerge, from the canopy, which is why they are called "emergents". Emergent trees usually have broad, waxy leaves that can withstand the incredibly hot sun and the 203–1,016 centimetres (80–400 in) of rain that might fall on them each year. Way, way down below, on the forest floor, the seedlings of other emergents wait their turn. When one of the adult emergents dies and leaves a space above the canopy, these seedlings start their race to the top, but just one or two will make it that far. The only animals at this emergent level are those with wings—that is, birds and insects.

Borneo rainforest

The most common emergent trees in the rainforests of Borneo are the dipterocarps. Of the world's 260 species of dipterocarp, 155 are native to Borneo. But the dipterocarps, which grow to a height of 37–64 metres (120–210 ft), are not the tallest trees of the Borneo rainforest. The silver-barked tualang tree, although less common, grows much taller.

Winged seeds *Like most emergents, dipterocarps have winged seeds that can use the wind to "fly" their seeds to the ground in another part of the rainforest.*

Oriental honey buzzard *This buzzard's main diet is bee, wasp and hornet pupae inside hives.*

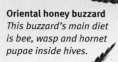

Tualang tree *The tualang, or honey bee tree, can reach 76 metres (250 ft), the height of a 20-storey building, with no branches below 30 metres (100 ft).*

Aerial view
The only way to see the top of the emergent trees, with their distinctive mushroom-shaped crowns, is from above.

Emergent

Pollinators *Tiny insects called thrips feed on the leaves of dipterocarps, but when the trees are in flower, they also act as pollinators.*

Bristleheads *These birds are insectivores, that is, their diet consists mainly of insects. Noisy flocks of bristleheads forage for beetles, grasshoppers and cockroaches.*

THE CLIMBING BEAR

The very rare sun bear is the champion climber among bears. But even the sun bear cannot climb high enough up the slippery tree trunk to reach the honeycombs on the tualang tree.

Honeycombs *Asian rock bees build their enormous 1.8-metre- (6-ft-) wide, disc-shaped honeycombs below the high branches of the tualang tree.*

Closed
Canopy

From above, the canopy looks like a sea of green treetops joined together in one mass, but trees in the canopy do not quite touch each other; there are gaps between them. The dense canopy can be up to 12 metres (40 ft) in depth and prevents most of the sunlight from reaching the layers below it. The branches of canopy trees are often covered with other plants that grow there, and lianas, or vines, hang down from the branches or tangle together. The canopy has more plant and animal species than any other layer in the rainforest, and thousands more undiscovered species may remain hidden in inaccessible rainforest canopies.

Moving around the canopy

Although they are more than 30 metres (100 ft) off the ground, monkeys move easily around the canopy. They scurry along branches and leap across the 1-metre (3-ft) gaps between the trees, using their tail for balance. Most of them have well-remembered routes to food sources, hiding places or easily jumped gaps.

Bat tunnels *These hammerhead bats take the same route every night through an area of the canopy where the vegetation has formed a tunnel.*

Crossing paths *The tracks created by the monkeys (red) cross the bat routes (blue), while the route of the springtails (yellow) is straight up the tree trunk.*

Canopy

Monkey tracks *The moustached monkey follows the well-trodden track where the moss, leaves, and twigs have been tramped down by many feet.*

Springtails *Although microscopic springtails spend much of their time feeding on leaf litter on the forest floor, they do climb to the canopy in search of fresh leaves.*

Sun-dappled
Understorey

The layer or storey beneath the canopy is called the understorey, and it receives less than 15 per cent of the sunlight that hits hits the canopy. With such limited sunlight, the understorey does not have the profusion or density of vegetation that the canopy has and it is therefore more open. The understorey starts at about 1.5 metres (5 ft) above the ground, and from this height to about 6 metres (20 ft), the plants are mainly shrubs. Above this shrub layer are low-growing trees such as palms that have very large leaves to catch what little sunlight there is. Above the palms are the young canopy trees on their way to the top and the moss-covered trunks of taller trees whose crowns are part of the canopy.

Barred leaf frog *This frog's long legs make it easy to climb to the understorey. Suction pads on its toes allow the frog to land on, and stick safely to, a leaf.*

Life in the half light

Although sunlight, required by plants for photosynthesis, is limited in the understorey, the plants there are protected from damaging solar radiation, drying winds and the heaviest of torrential rainfall. Compared with leaves of canopy and emergent trees, leaves in the understorey are not only larger but a deeper blue-green colour.

Waiting snake *Wrapped around a heliconia stalk, the eyelash viper waits patiently for prey to visit the flower . . . then it strikes.*

Understorey

Shafts of light
Only a few shafts of sunlight penetrate the small gaps between the trees in the canopy above to reach the sun-starved plants of the understorey.

Glasswing butterfly *This butterfly of the understorey lays its eggs on the leaves of a species of toxic nightshade. The caterpillars feed on the nightshade and take in some of the poison. Predators stay away from them.*

Honduran white bats *These tiny bats bite through the veins of a heliconia leaf until the leaf collapses into a V-shaped "tent" where they roost during the day, hidden from the sun and predators.*

Heliconia *The bright colours of the heliconia stand out against the green of the understorey and attract hummingbirds and bees.*

Dark,
Damp Floor

The rainforest floor, or ground level, is very dark and humid. It is here in this quiet, dark layer that the most vital activity for the rainforest takes place—the creation of nutrients, needed by all the plants. Rainforest soils are low in nutrients, but rainforests create their own nutrients by recycling all of the debris on the forest floor, including leaf litter, dead trees and other plants, dead animals and anything else that lies on, or falls to, the floor. Insects such as termites and some beetle species chew up debris. Fungi and bacteria break it down. The nutrients from this decomposed material are released into the top layer of the soil and feed the roots of all of the living rainforest plants.

Dead and alive

This tree may be dead and decaying, but it is alive with activity and is a home for many insects and small animals. Most importantly, this once-living tree will provide nutrients for the trees that are still growing.

1 **Fungi** *Digesting, decomposing and recycling are the main roles of fungi. Without them, the forest floor would be deep in debris.*

2 **Cup fungus** *Cookeina tricholoma not only looks good, it tastes good.*

3 **Bird's nest fungus** *The balls in the fungus are spores, which are flushed out by water, then start growing.*

4 **Coral snake** *The venomous red-, yellow- and black-banded snake spends most of its time hiding in the log.*

5 **Centipede** *Centipedes are carnivorous, so a fallen log, crawling with insects, is a perfect hunting ground.*

6 **Red fungus** *This fungus produces an antibiotic substance called cinnabarin.*

7 **Termites** *These key insects of the rainforest consume large amounts of wood and bark. Termite mounds are full of nutrients that enrich the soil.*

8 **Hyphae** *Fungi have threadlike cells called hyphae, which break down and absorb the cells of dead wood.*

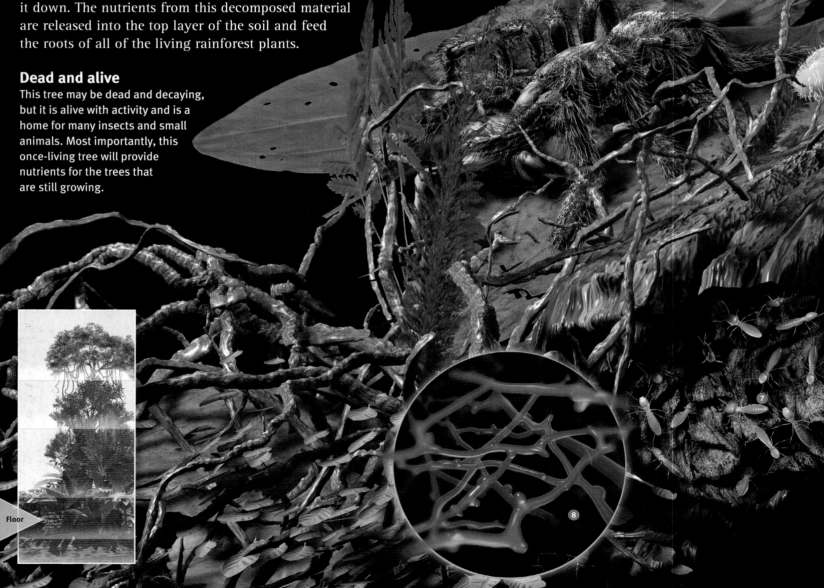

Floor

Running
River

Some of the world's longest rivers, such as the Amazon and its tributaries in South America and the Congo in Africa, run through rainforests. The rivers' waters are replenished by the large amounts of rain falling in these forests. Rivers provide a light-filled break in the dense vegetation of rainforests. Water in these rivers is described as "whitewater", which is in fact creamed-coffee coloured because of large amounts of sediment; "blackwater", which contains black tannins but is possibly the cleanest natural water in the world; and "clearwater", which is usually fast flowing. The different levels of acidity and minerals in each of these waters determine what plants grow in or beside the river.

Sepik River

The Sepik River flows from the central highlands of Papua New Guinea through the rainforest to the sea at Cape Girgir in the north. Freshwater plants in the highlands give way to salt-tolerant plants and mangroves as the Sepik nears the sea.

Sago palm *Native to Papua New Guinea, this useful palm is now found in many parts of South-East Asia, where its stem is used as a staple food and its leaves are used for thatching roofs.*

WEED-CLEARING WEEVIL

In the late 1970s, *Salvinia molesta*, an introduced water plant, was choking large areas of the Sepik River. A South American weevil was introduced and, by 1985, the weevil had cleared almost 260 square kilometres (100 sq mi) of the weed.

River

Jungle rice *This cereal grass grows on the swampy ground of the river bank.*

Aquatic plants *The submerged and above-water parts of these plants provide breeding sites, as well as food, for many insects and fish. Some of the plants have roots that fasten them to the river bed while others float free.*

Salt glands *The saltwater crocodile has special glands in its tongue that get rid of excess salt.*

Red-breasted paradise kingfisher *The carnivorous kingfisher dives straight down into the water to grab prey.*

Saltwater crocodile *The female crocodile lays up to 80 eggs in a mound nest on the river bank.*

Sepik rainbowfish *Rainbowfish (Glossolepis multisquamatus) thrive in the unpolluted waters of the Sepik, where they feed on small invertebrates in, or on top of, the water.*

Fertiliser *This free-floating aquatic fern is used as a fertiliser in rice paddies.*

Past, Present and
Future

Tropical rainforests have existed for hundreds of thousands of years. Since the arrival of human beings, rainforest areas have been declining. Human populations were initially small, but today, 200 million people live in rainforest regions. Since the 1980s, the scale of destruction has increased. More than 30 countries have now lost all of their rainforests. In one 15-year period (1980–95), an area of rainforest larger than Mexico was destroyed. Future predictions vary but we now know far more than we did in the past. A number of organisations, such as the United Nations and many environmental groups, are actively monitoring and protecting rainforests. Their future is in our hands.

Disappearing rainforests
In 1800, rainforest covered about 15 per cent of Earth's total land area; today less than 7 per cent of Earth's total land area is rainforest. Logging and deforestation destroy the rainforest habitat and threaten the wildlife that depend on it.

Present (2009) *There are now only 1.4 billion hectares (3.5 billion acres) of rainforest worldwide and the habitat of many animals has gone forever.*

Central America
Equator
Tropic of Cancer
South-East Asia
Tropic of Capricorn
Australia
South America
Africa

Past (1800) *In 1800, there were 3 billion hectares (7.1 billion acres) of rainforest worldwide. But already, by that date, the world's rainforests were in decline.*

Central America
Equator
Tropic of Cancer
South-East Asia
Tropic of Capricorn
Australia
South America
Africa

Special
Roots and Leaves

By adapting their roots and leaves, rainforest plants can flourish despite the difficult conditions they face. Emergent and canopy trees survive intense sun and torrential rain while plants at lower levels survive the lack of sunlight with leaves specially adapted to their circumstances. Rainforest soil is old and constantly damp, and its life-giving minerals have been leached out. Roots, therefore, are shallow, to absorb nutrients from decomposed litter in the top layer of the soil. With such shallow roots, the tallest trees then have to find a way to avoid toppling over.

LEAF ADAPTATIONS

If you pick up a leaf from the rainforest floor, you can usually tell which layer it fell from by its size, shape and colour.

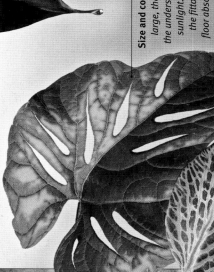

Drip tip *Leaves of canopy trees have drip tips that allow rain to drip off the leaf.*

Size and colour *By growing very large, the elephant ear leaf of the understorey can catch more sunlight. The red pigments in the fittonia leaf on the forest floor absorb more of the sun's rays in the red spectrum.*

Buttress roots

Emergent trees can grow to 76 metres (250 ft) and are very heavy, but their roots are too shallow to hold the huge trees upright in high winds. Special extensions from the trunk, called buttress roots, provide stability and support. The buttress roots also trap fallen leaves to provide and regulate additional nutrients for the main roots.

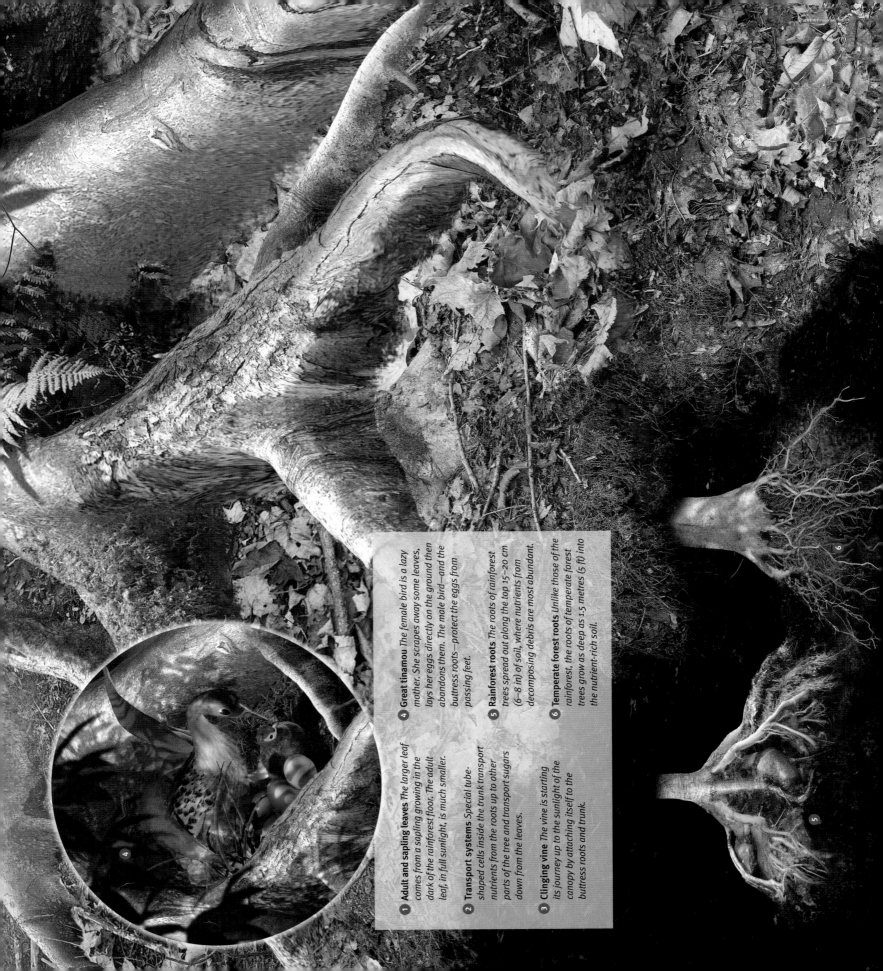

1 **Adult and sapling leaves** The larger leaf comes from a sapling growing in the dark of the rainforest floor. The adult leaf, in full sunlight, is much smaller.

2 **Transport systems** Special tube-shaped cells inside the trunk transport nutrients from the roots up to other parts of the tree and transport sugars down from the leaves.

3 **Clinging vine** The vine is starting its journey up to the sunlight of the canopy by attaching itself to the buttress roots and trunk.

4 **Great tinamou** The female bird is a lazy mother. She scrapes away some leaves, lays her eggs directly on the ground then abandons them. The male bird—and the buttress roots—protect the eggs from passing feet.

5 **Rainforest roots** The roots of rainforest trees spread out along the top 15–20 cm (6–8 in) of soil, where nutrients from decomposing debris are most abundant.

6 **Temperate forest roots** Unlike those of the rainforest, the roots of temperate forest trees grow as deep as 1.5 metres (5 ft) into the nutrient-rich soil.

Piggyback **Plants**

Growing in the soil of the rainforest floor has one huge
disadvantage for plants—at ground level there is little sunlight,
which the plants need for energy and growth. Some plants
solve this problem by growing on the branches of tall trees.
Their seeds germinate on the branch of a canopy or emergent
tree, where the growing plant gets all the sunlight it requires.
These plants, called epiphytes, "piggyback" on tall trees but do
not harm the trees. Vines, orchids, ferns and bromeliads are
common rainforest epiphytes, or piggyback plants.

VINES

Vines piggyback their
way to the sunlight using
a number of different
techniques: they hook on,
send out aerial tendrils or
twine around a support.

Hooks

Coiling tendrils

Twining

Sticky tendrils

Phalaenopsis orchid

Ant plant

Orchid

Bromeliads

The tough bromeliad leaves form a tank that
can hold 8 litres (2 gal) of water. This water
tank attracts many animals that come to
drink or to lay their eggs or larvae in
the water. The animal droppings, eggs,
larvae, dust and falling debris make a
mineral-rich "soup" that provides
nutrients for the bromeliad and its
resident community of animals.

Epiphytic fern

Piggyback clusters *The branches of some
canopy and emergent trees are covered with
different species of epiphytes.*

*Strong, waxy
bromeliad leaf*

Mouse opossum
The bromeliad tank provides
the tiny mouse opossum not
only with water, but also with
its favourite food—
insects.

Eyelash viper *The insects in
the water are of no interest to
the eyelash viper; the mouse
opossum is its target prey.*

Eggs and larvae
*Some mosquitoes
lay their eggs in a
"raft" on top of the
water tank, which
holds larvae of
other insects and
tadpoles.*

Strangler Figs

Strangler figs start their lives as piggyback plants, or epiphytes, high in the canopy. But the seed, dropped on a tree branch, sends thin roots down to the ground, and the life cycle of the strangler fig changes as it starts to grow from the ground up. That is why strangler figs are called hemiepiphytes ("half epiphytes"). Strangler figs also differ from true epiphytes because they are parasites—that is, they eventually kill the host tree. Tall strangler figs are common in all rainforests and are visited by many animal species. Their hollow structure and the small spaces created by the twisted latticework of its roots provide homes for insects, amphibians, reptiles, birds and rodents. The figs, which are produced several times a year, are an abundant source of food for thousands of rainforest animals.

Strangle and smother

In the final stages of its growth, the fig wraps itself so tightly around the tree that it strangles the trunk of the host tree. The fig's leaves smother the leaves of the host tree. The tree trunk is unable to grow outward and the leaves are unable to get the sun they need to produce energy for the tree to live. The host tree dies and rots away, providing nutrients for the strangler fig standing tall in its place.

Life inside a fig
Figs grow in clusters on short stems. Gall wasps use these figs as nurseries to incubate their young.

Seed The strangler fig seed begins to send shoots down to the ground. At this stage, the strangler fig grows very slowly.

Ground roots Rooted in the ground, the strangler fig grows more rapidly. The roots become thicker and wrap themselves around the trunk of the host tree.

5 The next generation The females fly off, tagged with pollen from the fig's male flowers, to lay their eggs in another fig.

4 The way out The male wasps then chew a new hole in the wall of the fig to let the pregnant females out, while they remain behind . . . and eventually die.

3 Male wasps The male wasps hatch first, bite a small hole in the female eggs, and inseminate the female wasp embryos.

1 Female gall wasp The pregnant female wasp, powdered with pollen from another fig, enters a hole in the bottom of the fig—and the hole closes behind her.

2 Pollination The wasp lays her eggs and the pollen she carries brushes off inside the fig.

Hollow core
The inside of a strangler fig is hollow. There is no solid timber, so loggers leave the strangler figs untouched.

Plant
Reproduction

In rainforests, below the canopy, there is no wind to blow plant pollen, so rainforest plants depend on birds, bats and insects to fertilise their female flowers with male pollen. Insects, nectar-eating bats and birds are the main pollinators as they move from flower to flower. Because of the fierce competition for light in the rainforest, seeds need to be dispersed as far away from the shade cast by the parent tree as possible. Mammals disperse seeds on their feet or when they pass undigested seeds, while birds and bats can fly the seeds well away from the parent plant.

Rafflesia

The rafflesia flower of Sumatra (*Rafflesia arnoldii*) is the world's largest flower, growing to more than 1 metre (3 ft) in diameter and weighing up to 10 kilograms (22 lb). It flowers for only 5–6 days every year and must attract pollinators during its brief flowering. The rafflesia flower gives off a smell like that of rotting meat, which attracts the carrion flies that transport its pollen.

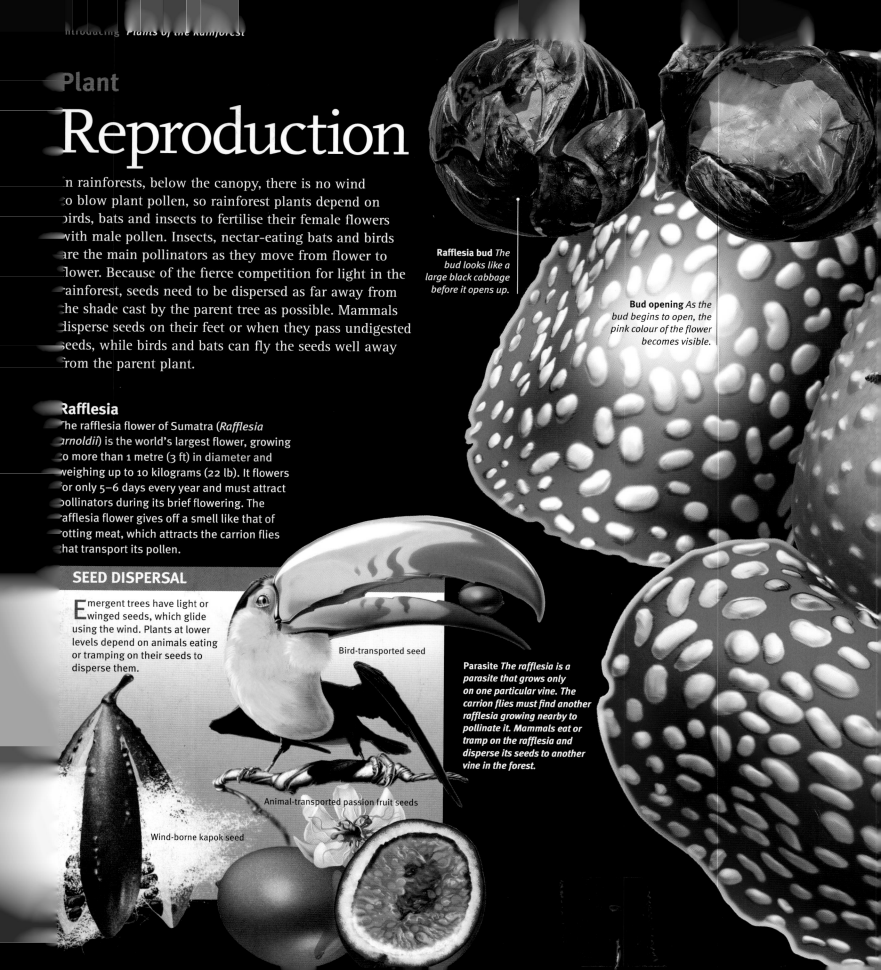

Rafflesia bud *The bud looks like a large black cabbage before it opens up.*

Bud opening *As the bud begins to open, the pink colour of the flower becomes visible.*

SEED DISPERSAL

Emergent trees have light or winged seeds, which glide using the wind. Plants at lower levels depend on animals eating or tramping on their seeds to disperse them.

Bird-transported seed

Parasite *The rafflesia is a parasite that grows only on one particular vine. The carrion flies must find another rafflesia growing nearby to pollinate it. Mammals eat or tramp on the rafflesia and disperse its seeds to another vine in the forest.*

Animal-transported passion fruit seeds

Wind-borne kapok seed

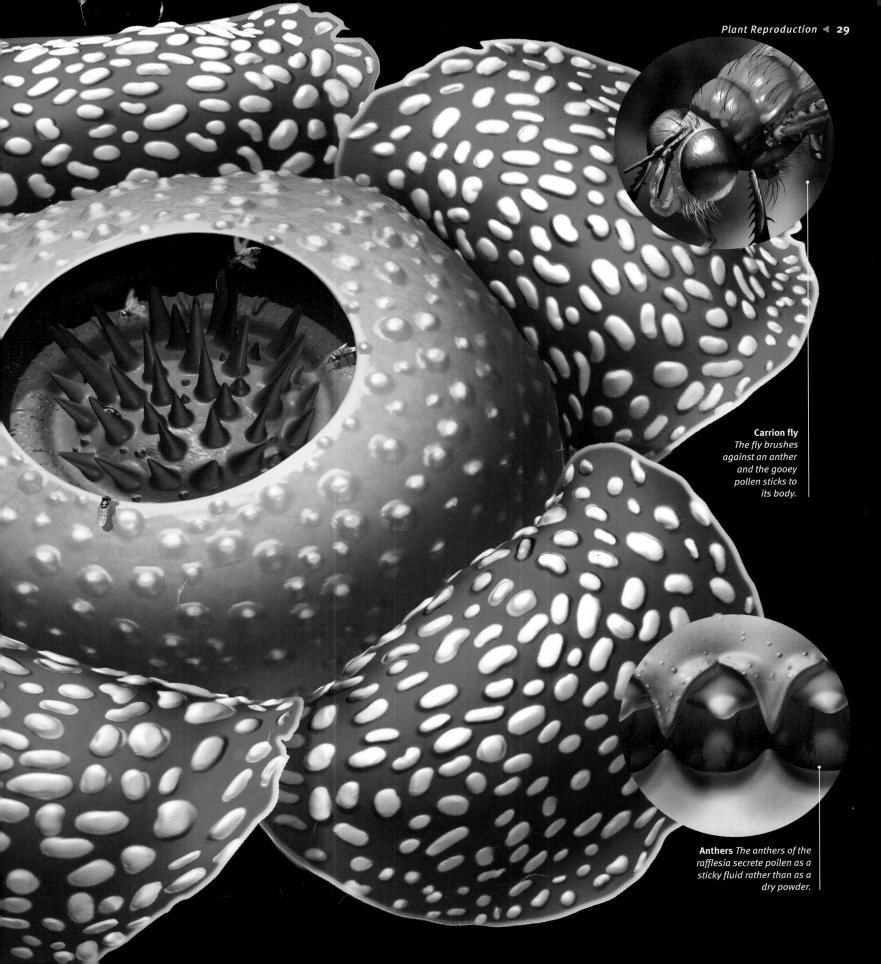

Carrion fly
The fly brushes against an anther and the gooey pollen sticks to its body.

Anthers *The anthers of the rafflesia secrete pollen as a sticky fluid rather than as a dry powder.*

Rainforest
Bounty

Although tropical rainforests cover only 7 per cent of Earth's land surface, they are home to more than half of Earth's 10 million plant and animal species. This wealth of species—called biodiversity—makes rainforests our most vital environment for species survival. Rainforests also help to "clean" the atmosphere by absorbing harmful carbon dioxide and adding oxygen to the atmosphere. The large amounts of water in and around rainforests make the local climate cooler and help to create rain clouds. Perhaps most important for those of us who do not live near a rainforest, many of the foods we eat every day and medicines we use for a wide range of illnesses, from headaches to cancer, come from rainforest plants.

HO_2

Water *Up to 10,920 millimetres (430 in) of rain falls each year on a rainforest. Some of this rain slowly trickles down to soak into the soil or flow into the river. But much of the water returns to the atmosphere as water vapour from the leaves.*

FOREST MEDICINE

Some rainforest plants contain oils and chemicals that can heal wounds and cure diseases. Drugs made from rainforest plants are used to treat diabetes, heart conditions, skin diseases, cancer and many other illnesses.

Quinine to fight malaria comes from cinchona tree bark.

Rosy periwinkle is used in cancer drugs.

Oxygen *During photosynthesis, carbon dioxide and water combine to form the plant's food, or sugars. The process also produces oxygen that the plant does not need, and this oxygen is released into the atmosphere.*

Carbon dioxide *The leaves in growing trees absorb carbon dioxide from the atmosphere to create the sugars needed for plant growth, in a process called photosynthesis. The carbon is stored in all parts of the tree.*

O₂

CO₂

Felling the Forests

For thousands of years, small patches of rainforest have been "slashed and burnt" by local people to clear enough land for a family farm. But these small farms are less of a problem today than the large-scale clearing of rainforests for commercial purposes. Logging companies clear fell; that is, they cut down all the trees in the area although only some will be used for timber. Large areas of rainforest are cleared for cattle ranches or for the planting of cash crops. Governments, too, can be responsible for felling rainforests to make way for roads or dams. An area of rainforest as big as Florida is destroyed each year, and the consequences are disastrous.

Here today, gone tomorrow

Rainforests are finely balanced, complex ecosystems where all the plants and animals depend on each other; that is, they are interdependent. Once that fine balance is disturbed by human beings, the ecosystem is affected. Even if only the tallest trees are cut down or if an area of rainforest on one side of the river is cleared, the rainforest ecosystem may not recover.

① **Fire** *Burning rainforest fires pollute the atmosphere for kilometres around with the carbon dioxide stored in the burning trees.*

② **Timber** *Not all rainforest trees make suitable timber, and many end up as wood pulp.*

③ **Crop failure** *Planted in poor soil, these crops soon fail.*

④ **River** *Without the rainforest trees to trickle rain slowly down to the soil, the rain washes much of the soil into the river.*

⑤ **Palm oil** *Money can be earned from biofuels like palm oil, so commercial plantations take the place of rainforest.*

Farming

Farmers plant new crops in nutrient-poor soil—without the ground litter from rainforest trees, there is no natural source of nutrients.

Virgin rainforest
Untouched by humans, virgin rainforest is a self-supporting environment providing all that it needs for healthy growth. It takes hundreds of years for a rainforest to grow to maturity— but only a few days to destroy it.

Clearing the land
After the rainforest trees are cut down, the remaining roots, stumps and undergrowth are burnt to clear the land, releasing the stored carbon into the atmosphere.

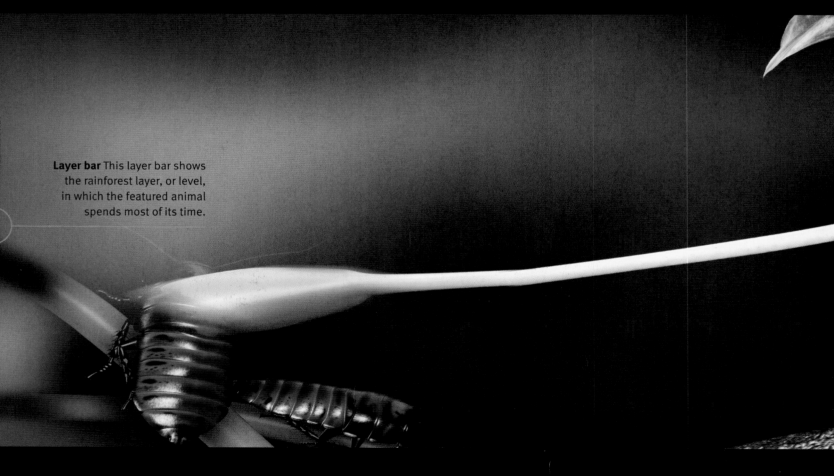

EMERGENT

CANOPY

UNDERSTOREY

GROUND

RIVER

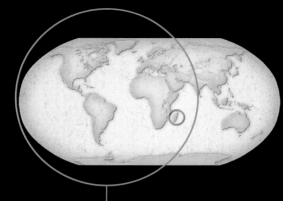

Locator map This map of the world's tropical rainforests shows you where the featured animal lives. Here the island of Madagascar is marked with a green circle.

PARSON'S CHAMELEON: THE FACTS

SPECIES: *Calumma parsonii*

WHERE: Understorey and canopy of Madagascar rainforest

RELATED SPECIES: 19 species of chameleons in genus *Calumma*

SIZE: The world's largest chameleon; 55–65 cm (22–26 in) long

WEIGHT: Up to 700 g (25 oz)

DIET: Mainly insects but also leaves, flowers, fruit, moss and twigs

REPRODUCTION: Female lays 25–50 eggs on the ground and covers them; female then abandons eggs, which can take 12–24 months to hatch

CONSERVATION STATUS: Not currently at risk

Fast facts Fast facts at your fingertips give you essential information on the animal species featured.

Layer bar This layer bar shows the rainforest layer, or level, in which the featured animal spends most of its time.

in *focus*

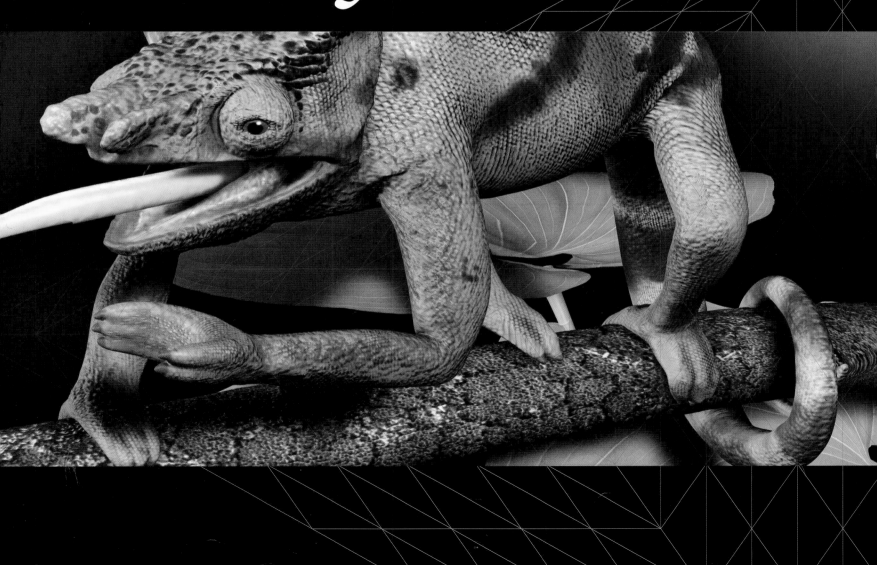

EMERGENT

CANOPY

UNDERSTOREY

GROUND

RIVER

Day and Night

Estimates suggest that, in an area of only 10 square kilometres (4 sq mi) of rainforest, there could be 125 species of mammals, 400 species of birds, 100 species of reptiles, 60 species of amphibians and 150 species of butterflies. With so many species sharing the same environment, animals use various means to avoid competing for food and space. In addition to spreading out among the layers of the rainforest and eating different seeds, fruit or meat, animals spread their waking and sleeping time over 24 hours. There is a great deal of activity in the rainforest every minute of the 24-hour day. Nocturnal animals are active only at night and sleep all day. Diurnal animals are up and about during the day and sleep at night. It is possible for animals to live in the same patch of rainforest but never to meet.

Sharing a tree

During the day, the male rhinoceros hornbill feeds fruit and insects to the female bird who is holed up in the tree trunk incubating her eggs. At night, the male returns to the canopy to sleep, and the tiny tarsier, the size of a human hand, comes out to eat. The nocturnal tarsier has such huge eyes that its skull is broader than it is long.

Termites *Although termites live in the dark, some species become bioluminescent, like fireflies, at night, and the termite mound is lit up like a Christmas tree.*

Fireflies *Night-flying fireflies produce light on the underside of their abdomens. The light from a firefly is "cold light", that is, all light and no heat.*

Bats *Flocks of bats, like these lesser short-nosed fruit bats, are the most common nocturnal animals, leaving their daytime roost to search for food at night.*

MANDRILL: THE FACTS

SPECIES: *Mandrillus sphinx*

HABITAT: Understorey and ground level of West African rainforest

RELATED SPECIES: Drill (*Mandrillus leucophaeus*)

SIZE: Height up to 76 cm (30 in)

WEIGHT: Males 20–28 kg (45–62 lb); females 11–12 kg (24–26 lb); occasional male can weigh up to 50 kg (110 lb)

DIET: Fruit, seeds, fungi, roots, insects, worms, frogs, lizards and small vertebrates

REPRODUCTION: Gestation period about six months; single young born every two years

CONSERVATION STATUS: Vulnerable

Living in
Groups

Some rainforest animals are loners; that is, they spend much of their lives alone and meet other animals of their species only during the mating season. However, many animals of the rainforest live in social groups and are rarely seen on their own. Group living offers the advantage of safety in numbers—if one animal fails to see an approaching predator, others in the group can sound a warning. Living in a group also makes it possible for a number of adults to protect the young and provides other opportunities to cooperate and socialise. Insects such as ants and termites, some bird species, apes and monkeys are the most common animal groups in the rainforest.

Living together

Mandrills, which are related to baboons, live together in groups of 15–50 individuals, headed by one adult male with a harem of adult females. The female young remain with the group, but on reaching adulthood, the males must leave the group to form their own. At certain times of year, a number of groups will join together in a large troop of up to 250 mandrills.

Mother and baby
The mother provides most of the care for her own infant but other females, and sometimes even males, will carry, groom or play with the young mandrill.

MIXED SPECIES FLOCKS

The gathering together of different species of birds in a large feeding flock is unique to tropical rainforests. The abundance of birds in the canopy shows there are enough insects or fruits to share.

Grooming *The bond between members of the group is made stronger by grooming each other. Mandrills use their fingers, lips and tongues when grooming the fur of other group members.*

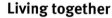

Communicating *Mandrills communicate using facial expressions, a wide variety of sounds and touch. The dominant male has the brightest coloured face and will "tension yawn" in anger to show fearsome teeth.*

EMERGENT

CANOPY

UNDERSTOREY

GROUND

RIVER

SUMATRAN ORANG-UTAN: THE FACTS

SPECIES: *Pongo abelii*

HABITAT: Understorey and canopy of North Sumatran rainforest

RELATED SPECIES: Bornean orang-utan (*Pongo pygmaeus*)

SIZE: Up to 1.5 m (5 ft) tall

WEIGHT: Up to 91 kg (200 lb)

DIET: Mainly fruit but also bark, leaves, insects and occasional small vertebrates

REPRODUCTION: Females, from the age of 15 years, give birth to single young (occasionally twins) with 8 years between births; gestation 245 days

CONSERVATION STATUS: Critically endangered

Swinging
Monkeys and Apes

Monkeys, apes, and their relatives are the best known animals of the jungle, or rainforest. There are more than 200 species, the majority of these being monkeys. All monkeys have tails, but only some New World monkeys of Central and South America have prehensile, or grasping, tails. Monkeys tend to gather in troops—often very noisy troops—and spend much of their time in the rainforest canopy. Apes have no tails and are usually larger than monkeys, with the 1.5-metre- (5-ft-) tall gorilla being the largest. Gorillas rarely climb, but the other apes—gibbons, chimpanzees and orang-utans—do climb and swing through the trees.

Sumatran orang-utan

The Indonesian words *orang* and *utan* mean "man of the forest", but orang-utans have adapted to moving through the forest much more effectively than any man. They are the largest arboreal, or tree-dwelling, mammals and rarely leave the trees. Often they climb—or scramble—up tree trunks, but sometimes they swing, hand-over-hand, using branches or vines. This movement is called brachiating.

Hands and feet
Orang-utans can brachiate using all four limbs since their feet are as flexible as their hands.

TAIL OR NO TAIL?

Some monkeys have tails strong enough to support their weight, leaving their hands free to grab food. The tail can also be used as a fifth limb when climbing. Apes have no tails, so they use other parts of their body to move through the rainforest.

Tail pad *The hairless pad under this monkey's tail is less likely to slip off the branch.*

Tough knuckles *Chimpanzees walk on their knuckles, not on the palms of their hands.*

PALE-THROATED THREE-TOED SLOTH: THE FACTS

SPECIES:	*Bradypus tridactylus*
HABITAT:	Canopy layer of South American rainforest
RELATED SPECIES:	Three other species of three-toed sloths
SIZE:	Up to 76 cm (2.5 ft)
WEIGHT:	Up to 8 kg (18 lb)
DIET:	Herbivorous; feeds on leaves, buds and twigs
REPRODUCTION:	Gestation period six months; gives birth to a single cub, which clings to its mother for a further 6 months
CONSERVATION STATUS:	Not currently at risk

Skilled
Climbers

A number of tropical mammals have evolved and adapted to arboreal life, that is, life in the trees of the rainforest. Many have a prehensile tail, which can be wrapped around a branch to prevent falls and to free the "hands" to grab food. The smaller the mammal, the higher it is likely to climb, since weight—and lack of wings—is a considerable disadvantage when climbing slender branches or lianas. Some of these arboreal mammals spend all of their lives and some spend only part of their lives in the trees. Apart from monkeys and apes, rodents, tree shrews and lemurs are the most common climbing mammals.

Slow moth *The sloth moth is the most visible of the insects that live in the sloth's shaggy coat. The moth lays its eggs in the sloth's dung on the forest floor.*

Hanging around

The strange-looking sloth spends almost all of its time in the canopy, clinging to a branch or moving—very slowly—hand over hand along the branch. Its front limbs are twice as long as its back limbs, which is ideal for hanging from a branch but makes it very clumsy on the ground, which it visits once a week, to defecate.

OTHER CLIMBERS

With specially adapted claws or tails, climbing mammals escape predators and pursue prey in the sunlit trees above the dark, tangled forest floor.

Anteater *The tamandua, or collared anteater, uses its prehensile tail when climbing.*

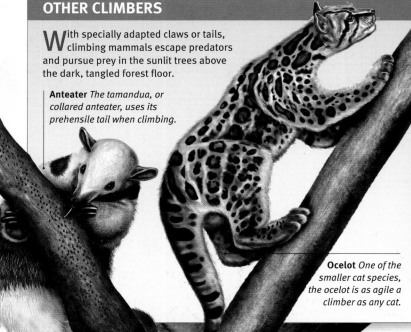

Ocelot *One of the smaller cat species, the ocelot is as agile a climber as any cat.*

EMERGENT

CANOPY

UNDERSTOREY

GROUND

Claws *The sloth's curved 10-centimetre (4-in) claws fasten it securely to the branch. The claws hang on even while the sloth sleeps, and after it dies.*

Green hair *In the damp rainforest, tiny green algae attach to the criss-crossed grooves in the sloth's coarse top hairs, giving the hairs their greenish tinge.*

EMERGENT

CANOPY

UNDERSTOREY

GROUND

RIVER

MALAYAN COLUGO: THE FACTS

SPECIES: *Cynocephalus variegatus*

HABITAT: Canopy layer of South-East Asian rainforests

RELATED SPECIES: Philippine colugo *(Cynocephalus volans)*

SIZE: 38 cm (15 in) head and body length; tail 25 cm (10 in)

WEIGHT: 1.5 kg (3.3 lb)

DIET: Herbivore; eats leaves, flowers, buds, fruit and pods

REPRODUCTION: Female gives birth to single young after 60-day gestation; baby colugo is very small and underdeveloped at birth; weaned at six months

CONSERVATION STATUS: Not currently at risk

Flyers and
Gliders

In rainforests, the ability to fly or glide at high levels and between tall trees is a distinct asset. The main difference between flying mammals and gliding mammals is the level of control over the flight. Bats are the only true flying mammals, with bones in their wings that allow the wings to flap and thus control height and direction. Gliding mammals do not have wings that flap. Instead, they have a membrane that opens like a parachute and depends on wind currents to control height and direction. The "flying lemurs" of the South-East Asian rainforest are not actually lemurs, and they do not actually fly. They are, in fact, gliding colugos. Other gliding mammals of the rainforest include the "flying" squirrels of Asia and the marsupial sugar glider of Australasia.

BATS

Bats' wings are really modified or adapted hands, which is why the name for the order to which all bats belong is Chiroptera, meaning "hand wing".

Gliding colugo

The colugo's gliding membrane stretches along both sides of the body from the neck to the tail. In order to glide, the colugo first has to climb high up in a tree since it can only glide down, not up. It leaps off one tree and glides downward to a neighbouring tree before climbing, leaping and gliding all over again. When not in use, the gliding membrane (called a patagium) hangs like loose skin down either side of the colugo's body.

AFRICAN FOREST ELEPHANT: THE FACTS

SPECIES: *Loxodonta cyclotis* or *Loxodonta africana cyclotis*

HABITAT: Ground level in West and West-Central African rainforests

RELATED SPECIES: African elephant; Asian elephant

SIZE: Up to 2.4 m (8 ft) tall; 7.5 m (24 ft) head and body length

WEIGHT: Males up to 5.4 tonnes (6 t); females up to 2.7 tonnes (3 t)

DIET: Leaves, twigs, branches, fruit and bark of many plants

REPRODUCTION: Female is pregnant for 22 months; gives birth to one calf weighing 90–120 kg (200–265 lb)

CONSERVATION STATUS: Vulnerable

Feet on the
Ground

Compared with other environments, like open savannah or plains, there are few large mammals at ground level in rainforests. Food for large mammals—large quantities of leaves and grass for herbivores or large prey species for carnivores—is not found on the dark rainforest floor. The ground is also a mass of vines, logs and forest litter, making a fast getaway—or a fast hunt—difficult for larger mammals. However, smaller mammals are more numerous and include rodents, pangolins, forest pigs and cat species. They feed on smaller prey, insects or the fruit and seeds that have fallen from the canopy.

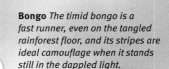

Push over *The elephant's trunk and tusks push over smaller trees and saplings, although larger trees in the elephants' path are safe.*

Bongo *The timid bongo is a fast runner, even on the tangled rainforest floor, and its stripes are ideal camouflage when it stands still in the dappled light.*

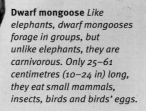

Dwarf mongoose *Like elephants, dwarf mongooses forage in groups, but unlike elephants, they are carnivorous. Only 25–61 centimetres (10–24 in) long, they eat small mammals, insects, birds and birds' eggs.*

New species

The African forest elephant was once thought to be a subspecies of the better known African elephant of the savannah. However, DNA tests on poached tusks revealed that they are two different species. Compared with African elephants of the savannah, forest elephants are smaller and have pinkish, straighter tusks—perhaps to avoid getting them hooked on vegetation. They also have a different skull shape and rounder ears.

EMERGENT

CANOPY

UNDERSTOREY

GROUND

RIVER

Crushing seedlings
New seedlings are no match for an elephant's foot and are crushed before they can take hold.

RAINFOREST "ARCHITECTS"

Over thousands of years, trampling as a herd along the same path, the elephants have created light-filled clearings that attract other ground-dwelling animals.

HARPY EAGLE: THE FACTS

SPECIES: *Harpia harpyja*

HABITAT: Emergent and canopy levels of Central and South American lowland rainforests

RELATED SPECIES: 50 species of eagles

SIZE: 1 m (40 in) from head to tail; 2.1-m (7-ft) wingspan

WEIGHT: Up to 8 kg (18 lb); females larger than males

DIET: Medium to large tree-dwelling mammals (mainly monkeys and sloths), large reptiles, rodents and other birds

REPRODUCTION: Usually two eggs laid but only the first egg to hatch survives; incubation 52–56 days

CONSERVATION STATUS: Threatened

Birds
Big and Small

Many of the largest birds of the rainforest are birds of prey whose domain is the emergent and canopy layers where they find and hunt their prey. However, some large rainforest birds, such as the cassowary of New Guinea and the great curassow of South America, spend all of their lives at ground level, feeding on fruit and seeds dropped from above. Small birds inhabit all levels of the rainforest, wherever the plants and insects that they feed on are found. Even those that spend most of their time on the forest floor will fly up to the canopy to call during the mating season. On the hottest days, birds of the canopy will often descend to a lower layer to find shade.

Danger approaching
The whole troop sees the harpy eagle approaching and starts howling in warning

Howling
The howls of the howler monkey can be heard up to 3.2 kilometres (2 mi) away.

Talons
The harpy eagle's talons are 13 centimetres (5 in) long and strong enough to carry prey up to half its own body weight.

SIZE COMPARISON

The regal king vulture is over five times longer but a massive 500 times heavier than the long-tailed hermit hummingbird.

King vulture *This scavenger eats the rotting remains of other animals.*

Hummingbird *Its tiny beak can reach the nectar deep inside the heliconia.*

The kill *The harpy eagle's talons grab the fleeing monkey.*

The target *The monkey that is the chosen prey tries to flee.*

Supreme hunter

Like all birds of prey, the harpy eagle has binocular vision, and its eyes are closely set, which makes it easier to judge distance. The harpy eagle also has an owl-like face disk that allows it to focus sounds. Its talons are lethal weapons. The howler monkeys recognise danger when they see the eagle but do not know which monkey will be the target until it is too late.

Selecting *Using its keen eyes, the eagle selects one monkey as its target.*

The approach *The harpy eagle flies at 80 kilometres an hour (50 mph) directly at the troop of howler monkeys.*

EMERGENT

CANOPY

UNDERSTOREY

GROUND

RIVER

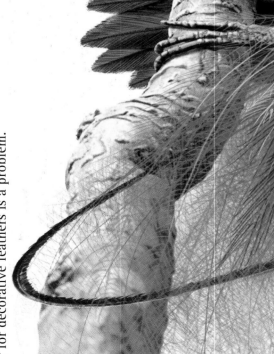

Quetzal *The resplendent quetzal, the national bird of Guatemala, gets its name from the word quetzalli, meaning "large brilliant tail feather." The tail feathers can be as long as 61 centimetres (2 ft).*

Flashes of Colour

Many birds of the rainforest are brilliantly coloured. Male birds are often more highly coloured than females and display their feathers to attract a mate. Most of these colourful birds are birds of the canopy. A large expanse of leaves means plenty of insects for the insect-eating birds, which often gather in noisy mixed flocks. The fruit-eating birds of the canopy include some of the larger colourful birds, such as toucans and hornbills. Unfortunately, however, these brilliant colours attract the attention of people, and poaching of rainforest birds for the pet trade or for decorative feathers is a problem.

BLUE BIRD-OF-PARADISE: THE FACTS

SPECIES: *Paradisaea rudolphi*

HABITAT: Canopy of Papua New Guinea montane rainforest

RELATED SPECIES: Six bird-of-paradise species of genus *Paradisaea*

SIZE: 30 cm (12 in) long, excluding the tail; up to 122 cm (4 ft) long including tail feathers

DIET: Mainly fruit

REPRODUCTION: The male abandons the female after mating. The female alone builds a nest in a low tree and incubates one or two eggs for 17–21 days.

CONSERVATION STATUS: Vulnerable

Blue bird-of-paradise

All male birds-of-paradise "display" to attract females, but the blue bird-of-paradise goes a stage further and performs acrobatics to get the attention of a female. Hanging upside down, the male blue bird-of-paradise spreads its wings, fluffs out its blue breast feathers and shows off its two long, black tail plumes. Males also gather together in a group to compete with each other. Each male performs in a display ground called a "lek".

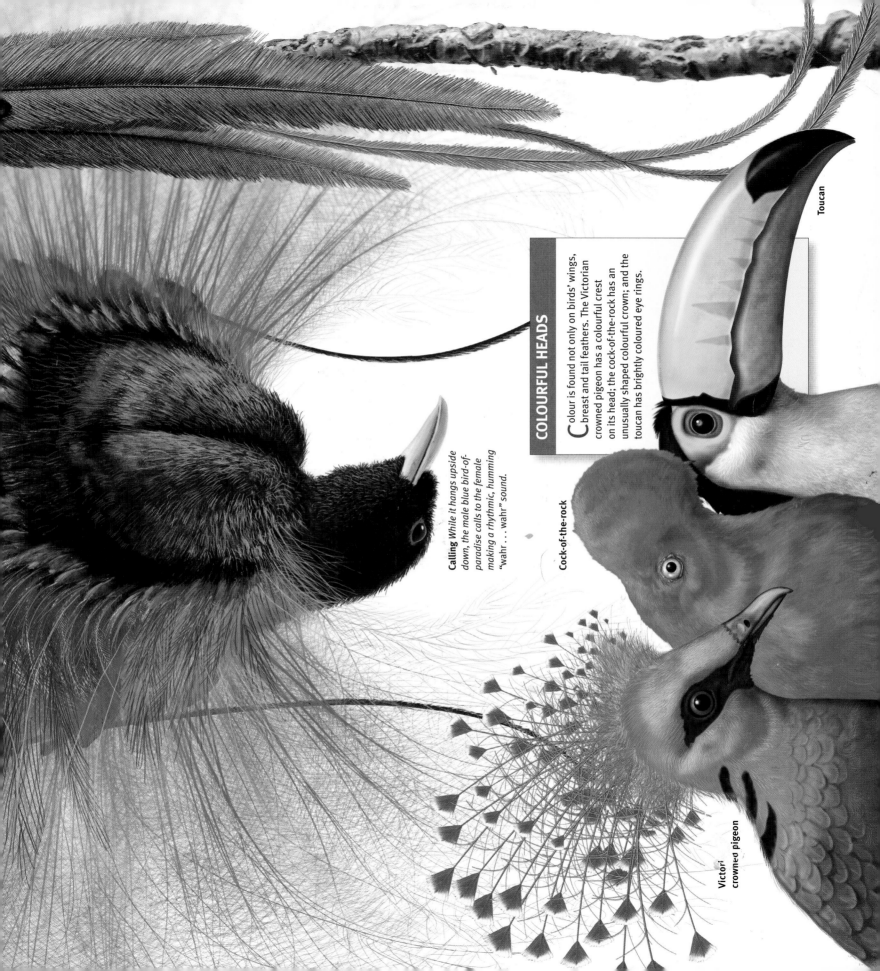

Calling *While it hangs upside down, the male blue bird-of-paradise calls to the female making a rhythmic, humming "wahr . . . wahr" sound.*

COLOURFUL HEADS

Colour is found not only on birds' wings, breast and tail feathers. The Victorian crowned pigeon has a colourful crest on its head; the cock-of-the-rock has an unusually shaped colourful crown; and the toucan has brightly coloured eye rings.

Toucan

Cock-of-the-rock

Victoria crowned pigeon

EMERGENT

CANOPY

UNDERSTOREY

GROUND

RIVER

ARMY ANTS: THE FACTS

SPECIES: *Eciton burchelli*

HABITAT: Mainly ground level in rainforests of Central and South America

RELATED SPECIES: 11 other species of *Eciton* ants

SIZE: 3–12 mm (0.1–0.5 in)

WEIGHT: Insignificant!

DIET: Carnivorous; feed mainly on other insects and arachnids

REPRODUCTION: Every three weeks, the wingless queen ant lays around 250,000 eggs, which are protected through the larval and pupa stage by worker ants

CONSERVATION STATUS: Not threatened

Armies of
Insects

Insects are the most numerous animals in the rainforests and can be found at every level. Unfortunately for the insects, there are many insectivores (birds, reptiles and mammals) at every level too. To stay safe, stick insects can camouflage themselves to look like leaves, and leaf bugs are almost indistinguishable from true leaves. There are butterflies with the most amazing colours and lantern bugs with snouts that look like tails on their heads. Beetles, wasps, bees and mosquitoes abound. But the most numerous insects of the rainforest are the thousands of species of ants that live in large colonies.

Ant colonies

Army ants live in large, well-organised colonies of up to 2 million ants. When the worker ants go out on swarm raids, they spread out in a fan shape to catch and subdue other insects, spiders or scorpions too weak or too slow to escape from the swarm.

Blue morpho *The blue morpho is actually brown! The top surfaces of the wings look blue because overlapping scales reflect blue light. The undersides of the wings, without reflecting scales, are a much drabber brown.*

Scorpion *Although much larger and with a nasty sting of its own, the scorpion is overwhelmed by a million stinging army ants. The ants will tear the scorpion's body into small pieces and carry it back to the rest of the colony.*

Worker ants The almost blind ants have hook-shaped mandibles that cannot cut so are used to tear off bits of prey. Worker ants also have hooks on their ankles to grip each other to form a bivouac or "nest" from their own bodies.

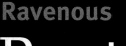

species: *Calumma parsonii*

HABITAT: Understorey and canopy of Madagascar rainforest

RELATED SPECIES: 19 species of chameleons in genus *Calumma*

SIZE: The world's largest chameleon; 56–66 cm (22–26 in) long

WEIGHT: Up to 709 g (25 oz)

DIET: Mainly insects but also leaves, flowers, fruit, moss and twigs

REPRODUCTION: Female lays 25–50 eggs on the ground and covers them; female then abandons eggs, which can take 12–24 months to hatch

CONSERVATION STATUS: Not currently at risk

Ravenous
Reptiles

The only reptiles that are confined to one particular level of the rainforest are turtles and crocodiles. Snakes and lizards inhabit all levels of the rainforest. Some snakes spend the day basking in the sunlight of the canopy but spend the night hanging by their tails from branches in the understorey, waiting for prey. Other kinds of snakes never leave the ground. There are more than 2,000 species of rainforest lizards, ranging in size from the 3-metre- (9-ft-) long carnivorous komodo dragon to tiny insect-eating geckos.

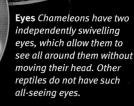

Eyes *Chameleons have two independently swivelling eyes, which allow them to see all around them without moving their head. Other reptiles do not have such all-seeing eyes.*

Unusual lizards
More than two-thirds of the world's chameleons live on the island of Madagascar. Chameleons have a number of unique features, including 3-D sight and the world's fastest tongue.

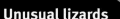

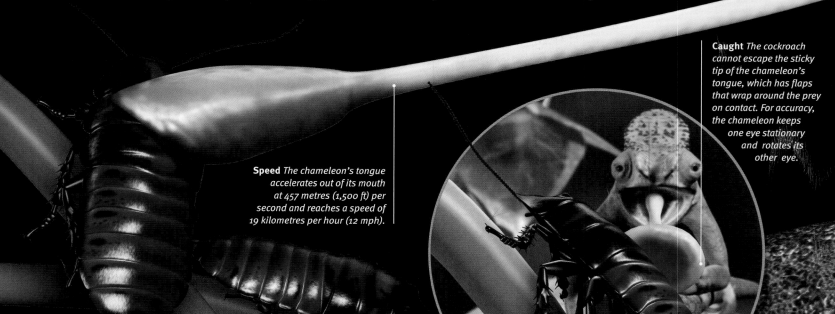

Caught *The cockroach cannot escape the sticky tip of the chameleon's tongue, which has flaps that wrap around the prey on contact. For accuracy, the chameleon keeps one eye stationary and rotates its other eye.*

Speed *The chameleon's tongue accelerates out of its mouth at 457 metres (1,500 ft) per second and reaches a speed of 19 kilometres per hour (12 mph).*

Tongue *Muscles contract and catapult the rolled-up tongue, 1–2 times the chameleon's body length, out of its mouth.*

Changing colour *The layers of skin under the top layer contain special colour-reflecting cells that allow the chameleon's skin to change colour according to mood, temperature and light intensity.*

Frog Life

Water is in plentiful supply in rainforests, so it is not surprising that the sight—and sounds—of many frog species are common. Most, but not all, rainforest frog species lay eggs that develop into tadpoles, which live in water at all levels of the rainforest until they eventually metamorphose into adult frogs. The most remarkable rainforest frogs are the very colourful poison arrow or poison dart frogs of Central and South America. Their stunning colours are a warning to possible predators that they are toxic. Their skin is poisonous, not because of any poison cells in the skin layers, but because of the toxins in the ants and mites that they eat.

Granular poison arrow frog

This tiny frog is not much larger than the top joint of a human thumb. Despite its size, the female frog makes the difficult climb from the ground to the canopy, transporting her tadpoles on her back up to the water in a bromeliad plant. She returns regularly to feed the tadpoles with her unfertilised eggs.

GRANULAR POISON ARROW FROG: THE FACTS

SPECIES: *Dendrobates granuliferus*

HABITAT: From ground to canopy layers of rainforests in Costa Rica and Panama

RELATED SPECIES: 41 other species of poison frogs in genus *Dendrobates*

SIZE: Less than 19–22 mm (1 in) long

WEIGHT: 3.2 g (1/10 oz)

DIET: Insectivore; eats mainly ants and mites

REPRODUCTION: 2–5 eggs hatch after 19 days and are transported to water; tadpoles metamorphose (become frogs) in 90–200 days

CONSERVATION STATUS: Vulnerable

1 **Croaking frog** *Only male frogs croak—to attract females and to warn off other males. An air sac in the frog's mouth makes the sound from the vocal cords louder.*

2 **Glass frog** *This frog is transparent and lays its eggs on the underside of a leaf over water. When the tadpoles hatch, they drop into the water below.*

3 **Pac-man** *The horned frog is also known as the Pac-man frog because its head is all mouth. This frog is carnivorous and feeds on other frogs.*

4 **Poison arrow** *The golden poison arrow frog is so poisonous that an arrowhead rubbed against its back will cover the arrow in enough poison to kill a large animal.*

ENDANGERED SPECIES: THE FACTS

EXTINCT: Since 1994, 30 species of rainforest animals have become extinct

EXTINCT IN THE WILD: In the past six years, 4 species of rainforest animals have become extinct in the wild; these animals can still be seen in captivity

CRITICALLY ENDANGERED: 650 rainforest animal species are critically endangered; the probability of extinction within 10 years or three generations is 50 per cent

ENDANGERED: 1,200 rainforest animal species are endangered; there is a 20 percent chance of extinction within 20 years

VULNERABLE: More than 2,000 rainforest animal species are vulnerable, that is, close to being endangered

Going, Going, Gone

The future of almost 5,800 species of rainforest mammals, birds, reptiles, amphibians and insects is at risk and some of these species are heading towards extinction. Sometimes natural disasters, parasites or invasive species can put animal populations at risk, but human activity is the main reason that an increasing number of animals are endangered. Some animals, such as elephants, large cats and birds, are hunted for their tusks, furs, or feathers. Exotic reptiles, some monkeys and apes, and colourful birds are captured for the pet trade. But the single most important cause of endangerment is loss of habitat. With nowhere to rest, breed or sleep and with no food to eat, the animals die.

Monitoring

The World Conservation Union is one organisation that monitors endangered species by counting populations. Its annual Red List gives advance warning to governments and other organisations on species at risk, allowing them to take action before it is too late.

Bornean orang-utan *Poaching for the pet market and forest burning have endangered this orang-utan.*

Queen Alexandra's birdwing *The world's largest butterfly has been endangered for the past 20 years.*

Bongo *The bongo has vanished from the rainforests of Uganda but is not at risk elsewhere in Africa.*

Sumatran tiger *Habitat loss and hunting have reduced the numbers of this critically endangered tiger to 250 adults.*

Golden lion tamarin *Once critically endangered, numbers have increased to 1,000 but this monkey is still endangered.*

Golden parakeet *Trapping and habitat loss have endangered this bird of the Amazon Basin.*

Mitu mitu bird *This Brazilian rainforest bird is now extinct in the wild, but there are a few left in captivity.*

Gastric brooding frog *No one will ever see this frog giving birth to live young through its mouth; it has been extinct since the 1980s.*

EMERGENT

CANOPY

UNDERSTOREY

GROUND

RIVER

African elephant
Both African elephant species are vulnerable because of the ivory trade and habitat loss.

Harpy eagle *This eagle was under threat 20 years ago, but populations are increasing.*

Dark flying fox
This bat has been extinct since the 1860s.

Mountain gorilla
This gorilla is critically endangered—there were only 325 mountain gorillas left at the last count.

Blue poison frog
Poaching for the pet trade and forest fires have made this frog vulnerable.

Kaua'i 'O'o bird
Assumed to be extinct since the last pair was sighted in the 1980s.

Three-banded armadillo *Mining, farming and hunting have killed more than 30 per cent of the population so that now this armadillo is under threat.*

Asia

The rainforests of Asia stretch as far west as India but the largest areas of remaining rainforest are concentrated in Malaysia, Indonesia and Borneo in South-East Asia.

Iban The Iban of Borneo live as a group in longhouses and fish the local waters.

Penan Wild pig is a staple food for the Penan people of Borneo.

Rainforests of the World

The people who live in the world's rainforests depend on the plants and animals in their environment. They have carefully conserved these resources over many generations.

Chimbu Men and boys paint their faces for celebrations, or sing-sings, in Papua New Guinea.

Australia and Papua New Guinea

Rainforests in Australia are limited to a few remnants on the north-east coast, but 55 per cent of the land area of Papua New Guinea is rainforest.

Africa

Although there are 37 African countries with some rainforest, the largest area of rainforest is in four countries of the Congo Basin—the Democratic Republic of Congo, Gabon, Cameroon and Congo.

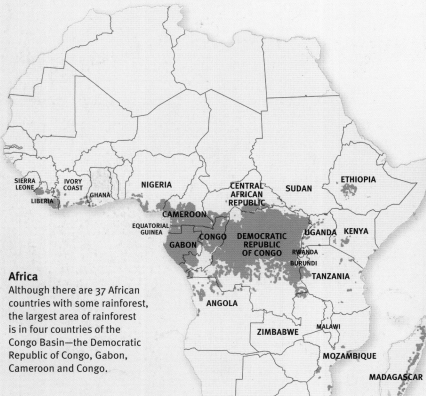

Mbuti Boys of the Mbuti tribe in the Democratic Republic of Congo dance in grass skirts during a ceremony.

Mexico and Central America

The rainforests of Central America stretch from southern Mexico right through to Panama. El Salvador is the only Central American country with almost no rainforest.

Kuna The Kuna women of Panama wear distinctive red headscarves.

Huaorani Hunting with blow guns is a traditional—and effective—technique for the Huaorani men of Ecuador.

South America

The Amazon rainforest, which spreads 6.5 million square kilometres (2.5 million sq mi) across Brazil and eight other South American countries, is the world's largest tropical rainforest.

Yanomami Women in southern Venezuela and northern Brazil collect termites on banana leaves to add to their staple diet of plantain.

TYPES OF RAINFOREST

Equatorial evergreen rainforests, close to the Equator, receive more than 203 centimetres (80 in) of rain spread evenly through the year. These are low-land forests with very dense canopies. Tropical moist forests, which can grow in highlands 1,525 metres (5,000 ft) above sea level, are further away from the Equator and receive 127 centimetres (50 in) of rain during the wet season. In the cooler dry season, many trees lose their leaves, so the canopy is less dense.

Tropical moist forest Gaps in the canopy allow sunlight to reach—and plants to grow on—a Mexican rainforest floor.

Equatorial evergreen forest There are no seasons and the sun shines for the same number of hours every day in the rainforest of Borneo.

Kayapó One of the Amerindian tribes of Brazil, the Kayapó use sophisticated techniques such as soil fertilisation and rotation of crops to manage the rainforest in which they live.

Glossary

adaptation The gradual change of a body part, over many generations, to make it more suitable or useful for a specific situation or environment. A prehensile tail that can grip branches is an adaptation in some monkey species.

algae Simple plantlike organisms with no stems, roots or leaves that grow in water or very humid conditions. Algae include the microscopic algae that form green pond scum (or stick to a sloth's hair) and large seaweeds.

amphibian An animal whose life cycle usually includes an early stage (as larva or tadpole) of living in water and an adult stage when it lives on land. Frogs, toads, newts and salamanders are all amphibians.

anther The part of the male organ of a flower that produces pollen.

arboreal Living in trees, from the French word *arbor,* meaning "tree". The opposite of arboreal is terrestrial, which describes animals that live at ground level.

biodiversity Short for "biological diversity", which is measured by the number of different species of plants and animals in an environment.

biofuel A fuel produced from natural, often plant, sources that are renewable and are also carbon neutral (the carbon emitted during use is balanced by the carbon absorbed by new plants). Palm oil and ethanol, made from sugar, are two common biofuels.

bioluminescence The emission of light by some animals including insects and fish. Light comes from a substance called luciferin in special cells.

brachiate To move through trees by swinging from branch to branch or vine to vine using hands and arms.

buttress roots Extensions that project from the trunks of emergent trees to provide support and stability.

canopy The spreading branches and treetops that provide a cover for the layers below.

carbon dioxide A gas in the atmosphere that is given out by burning fossil fuels (like wood and coal), and by plants and animals when they breathe out.

carbon sink Living things that soak up carbon from the atmosphere rather then emitting it. Plants take in carbon during photosynthesis and store it, temporarily, in trunks, roots and leaves. If plants are burnt, they become carbon emitters, not carbon sinks.

carnivore An animal that eats the meat or flesh of other animals.

cash crop A crop that is sold for money and not consumed by those growing the crop.

cell The basic unit from which all plants and animals (including humans) are made. Each cell has a specific function or purpose.

clear fell To cut down all the trees in one area so that the land is totally cleared and no trees remain standing.

crown The leaves or foliage at the very top of a tree. Also the top part of a bird's head.

display To show off, or exhibit, features (such as feathers) to a possible mate.

diurnal Active during the day and sleeping at night.

drip tip The pointed tip of a leaf that allows water to drip off the end of the leaf.

ecosystem A community of plants and animals and the environment in which they live.

embryo An animal in the early stages of growth before birth or hatching.

emergent A very tall tree that grows higher than other trees and rises (or emerges) above the level of the canopy.

endangered A species of animal or plant in danger of becoming extinct in the near future.

epiphyte A plant that grows on tree branches and trunks, not in the soil. An epiphyte makes its own food and does no harm to the tree that it grows on.

extinct A species of animal or plant that no longer exists because the last individual has died.

floor Another name for the ground level in a rainforest.

forage To browse, graze or hunt for food.

fungus An organism that cannot make its own food so feeds on and breaks down plant and animal materials.

germinate The stage in a plant's life cycle when the stem and roots sprout from the seed.

gestation Stage before birth when a young animal grows inside its mother.

habitat The environment or place where an animal or plant lives and grows.

hemiepiphyte A plant that spends half or part of its life as an epiphyte.

herbivore An animal that eats only plant materials such as flowers, fruits, nuts, leaves and bark.

hyphae Threadlike elements that make up the body of a fungus and attach to, break down and decompose plant cells.

incubation To sit on eggs and use the heat of the body to keep the eggs warm enough to hatch.

insectivore An animal or plant that eats insects.

interdependent A group of plants or animals sharing a habitat and depending on each other for life or survival.

invertebrates Animals without backbones (or spines), such as insects and spiders.

larvae The undeveloped, newborn and wingless forms of insects that hatch from the eggs before growing into pupa. *See* pupa.

layers Different vertical levels within a rainforest from the top or emergent layer down through the canopy and understorey to the ground layer.

liana A woody vine that roots in the soil.

litter The top layer of decomposing or decayed matter (animal and plant) on the rainforest floor.

mandible One of the mouthparts or jaws of an insect or invertebrate; the lower jaw of a vertebrate. Mandibles are used to hold, rip or bite food.

membrane A thin, flexible layer of skin or tissue that can be opened for gliding.

metamorphose To change to a different physical form after birth or hatching. A caterpillar metamorphoses into a butterfly; a tadpole metamorphoses into a frog.

minerals The chemical elements needed by all living things. The major minerals required by plants are potassium, phosphorus, calcium and magnesium, which are transported in water from the roots to other parts of the plant.

monitoring Observing carefully and reporting or warning on the results of the observation.

nocturnal Active at night and asleep during the day.

nutrients Substances that provide the essential "foods" needed for life. Plant nutrients include the nonminerals (oxygen, carbon and hydrogen) that come from air and water, as well as the minerals that come from the soil. *See* minerals.

ovary The part of a plant that contains the female cells and becomes the fruit after it is pollinated. The reproductive part of a female animal where the eggs or embryos are formed.

parasite A plant or animal that lives and feeds on another plant or animal, damaging or destroying the host in the process.

photosynthesis The process by which a plant takes in sunlight, water and carbon dioxide to make the plant's food or sugars.

poaching The illegal hunting, trapping and killing of protected animals.

pollinator An animal that transfers male pollen to female flowers.

pollute To contaminate an environment, making it harmful or unfit for living things. Water, air and soil can all be polluted, often by human action.

predator An animal that kills and eats other animals that are its prey. *See* prey.

prehensile tail A tail that is adapted to grasping or wrapping around a support such as a branch.

prey An animal that is hunted and killed by another animal (called a predator).

pupa The stage of development of an insect when it develops inside a cocoon or other protective coating before emerging in adult form.

roost To rest or sleep on a perch or other suitable high place.

sapling A young tree or shrub that has only started to grow to its full mature height.

seedling A very young plant that has just started growing from the seed.

slash and burn Destruction of areas of rainforest by cutting down (slashing) the trees then setting fire to (burning) the remaining stumps and debris.

subspecies A subdivision of a species into two or more groups usually based on geographic distribution. For example, the species *Gorilla gorilla* is divided into two subspecies: *Gorilla gorilla gorilla*, the western lowland gorilla, and *Gorilla gorilla graueri*, the eastern lowland gorilla.

talon The large claw of a bird of prey.

thrip Tiny winged insect that sucks on the sap of plants and often damages them.

toxic Poisonous and likely to harm any plant or animal consuming it.

understorey The rainforest layer beneath the canopy and above the ground.

vertebrates Animals with backbones or spines. Mammals (including humans), birds, reptiles, amphibians and fish are all vertebrates.

virgin rainforest Rainforest still in its natural state, with no human interference.

Index

Credits

The publisher thanks Puddingburn for the index.

Key t=top; l=left; r=right; tl=top left; tcl=top centre left; tc=top centre; tcr=top centre right; tr=top right; cl=centre left; c=centre; cr=centre right; b=bottom; bl=bottom left; bcl=bottom centre left; bc=bottom centre; bcr=bottom centre right; br=bottom right

ILLUSTRATIONS
Front cover Christer Eriksson (main); Contact Jupiter/Yvan Meunier (support)
Back cover Peter Bull Art Studio t,bl; Contact Jupiter/Yvan Meunier bc
Spine Peter Bull Art Studio
Peter Bull Art Studio 8-9, 10-11, 12-13, 14-15, 16-17, 18-19, 20-1, 30-1, 32-3, 36-7, 38-9, 40-1, 42-3bl, ct, br, 44bl, 46-7, 48-9, 50-1bl, bc, br, 52-3, 54-5, 58-9
Christer Eriksson 42-3, 44-5, 50-1
Contact Jupiter (Yvan Meunier) 22-3, 24-5, 26-7, 28-9, 56-7
Guy Troughton 45 tr

MAPS
Andrew Davies; Map Illustrations

PHOTOGRAPHS
ALA = Alamy; CBT = Corbis; GI = Getty Images; iS = istockphoto.com; MP = Minden Pictures; NPL=Nature Picture Library
10bcl MP **14**cl iS **20**bl, c GI **21**bc ALA tr GI **27**br NPL **60**br, tcl, tr GI cr CBT **61**bl MP br CBT c iS cl, tl GI tr NPL

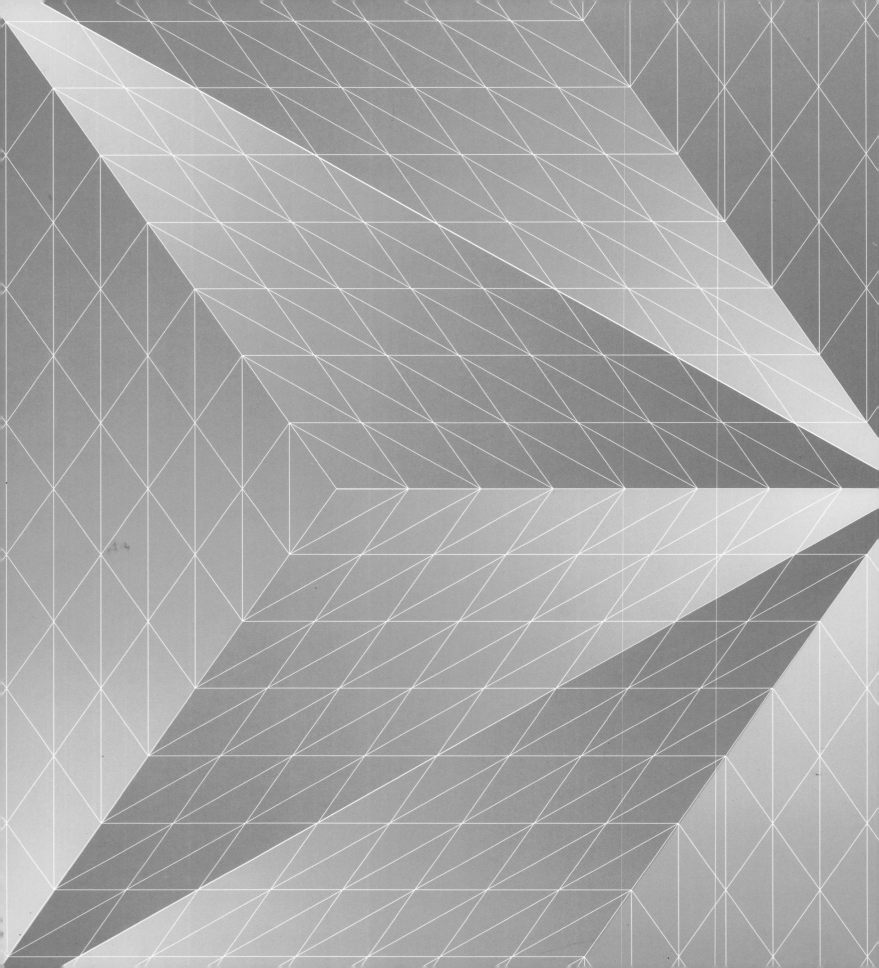